sock monkeys

(200 out of 1,863)

Arne Svenson + Ron Warren

IDEAL
WORLD
BOOKS

for Charles
and
for Joshua

FOREWORD

When in 1915 George Nelson, a Rockford, Illinois, manufacturer, patented a knit cotton work sock with a reinforced red heel, it's doubtful that he considered its divine suitability as a monkey's protruding lips or blushing rear end. Nevertheless, sometime around the Great Depression one unknown visionary, building on a long tradition of sock dolls, improvised the minimal snipping and seaming that would transform this lowly article of clothing into a jocular icon: one sock would define the body from head to toe, with the red heel as rump; from the other sock, the red heel would be cut out to form the mouth, with the ankle apportioned into arms and tail, and the toe into a hat. This know-how was passed along by word of mouth until 1953, when the Nelson Knitting Company, to satisfy inquiries and promote sales of the socks, published a standard pattern for making a Red Heel Sock Monkey.

With these simple directions, amateur sewers across the nation gained confidence that they too could stitch a companion for a child or loved one. A sock monkey craze had begun. The individual makers, whether by skill or lack of it, imbued their creations with specific characteristics and identities, using scarcely more than buttons, thread, and the occasional jingle bell.

Ron's foray into collecting vintage sock monkeys began in 1985 when his friend Josh discovered one in a rural West Virginia shop. Having no idea what it was, he brought the creature home to Ron, who explained the origin and significance of these stuffed animals. To show Josh that each monkey is unique, Ron vowed to find another. Their variety proved irresistible, and at present, having combed the offerings of numerous flea markets and thrift stores, he has 1,863 sock monkeys.

A mutual friend told Arne about the collection, knowing that he would be fascinated not only by the monkeys themselves, but by the astounding number Ron had acquired. Upon entering the room where the sock monkeys are kept, Arne was overwhelmed by the vision before him: draped over tables and chairs, piled in boxes, and strewn on the floor were hundreds and hundreds of little woven bodies. Only half-joking, Arne proposed to photograph each and every monkey. The next day, a bag of thirty sock monkeys in hand, Ron arrived at the studio. Arne set about to record them in the manner of classic studio portraiture: each monkey flatteringly lit, cropped at the shoulders, eyes to the camera. The series is shot in black-and-white, the optimal medium for highlighting each monkey's expressiveness. Focusing on the eyes and facial characteristics, Arne seeks out the same indicators of personality that he would with a human subject.

After hearing numerous tales and reminiscences from friends who saw the portraits, we began to invite authors to write stories inspired by their favorite sock monkey photograph. The results range from the sweet to the frightening, the sublime to the bizarre. Where Penn Jillette envisions a "bad monkey wammerjammer" who was "sewn in a crossfire hurricane of needles and pins," Isaac Mizrahi imagines Madam Ludmilla Yakushova, a retired prima ballerina who teaches a master class.

Every chance he gets, Arne continues to photograph the collection. And Ron, every chance he gets, still acquires sock monkeys.

Arne Svenson
Ron Warren

Sewn Under a Bad Sign

Bad monkey wammerjammer. Sewn in a crossfire hurricane of needles and pins. An imaginary friend's howlings in the driving rain of the washing machine. Don't you wanna live with me?

Look at my eyes. Look at them. I told you to look in my eyes! These aren't giggly jokey eyes to make babies giggle. My button eyes are like a shark's eyes. Buttons from a sharkskin suit. My eyes have been fiddled with by a hustler. Nervously tapped by a bad man. My eyes are worn right in the center from the tapping of a diamond pinky ring. It was his gambler's "tell." When the owner of that expensive, but still very cheap suit was lying, he'd *click click click click* his flawed diamond against the buttons of his suit jacket. And he was lying all the time. *Click click click click click.* Those buttons are my eyes! They were always my eyes. They saw everything from the coat of a wheeler-dealer, Mr. Ferris, the big wheel down at the carnie. Doctor, my eyes! My eyes have seen the pain of a lying diamond. Black eyes. No emotion. Predator. Predator sock monkey. Bad monkey.

Look at my skin. It's not born from a clean, new sock. No way. This is a sock that has been used. Look at my mouth. My mouth sheathed a real toe. A man's toe. It rammed against the end of a steel-toe boot. That makes a monkey tough. Very tough. There's human blood in my mouth. Blister blood. And foot sweat. I taste foot sweat all the time. Lumberjack foot sweat. I'm worn. I've been around. My mouth has walked 47 miles of barbed wire. Bad monkey.

And the heel of that sock skin. You know where that is. You know what that heel became don't you? You have your little baby names for it, but you know what it really is. Yup, it's that heel that kicked me in the you-know-where. My very fiber is a kick in the behind. That's what I am. Bad. That's me. Kick it. Bad monkey.

Bad to the nylons stuffing my innards. I'm not stuffed with children's old PJs. No way. And I'm not stuffed with sensible modest panty hose that got, oh pshaw, a run. No! I'm stuffed with nylons. Nylon stockings. Modern petroleum chemical artificial nylons that held on with a black lace garter belt around the legs of a woman. A woman. A woman with legs up to there. Not a lady. Not a child. A woman. That's what my stuffing is. My stuffing smells like cheap perfume. Cheap perfume that was put on those shapely upper thighs. That's not where you put perfume. Bad monkey.

Lumberjack sock stuffed with women's nylons. Yeah, the old lady washed them. She washed me all. I was created clean, but that smell is deep. Deep. Deep. It's a smell of the soul, and my soul is a lumberjack's sole. I've been worn. It's walked miles to smell those nylons of my innards.

Hustler eyes, lumberjack skin, the heart of a woman's legs, and a grandmother's spoiling love. I got it all, baby. I got it all, my little baby boy. Drool on me. Grab me. Carry me. Rip me apart. I'm a bad monkey.

The little fool calls me "Dickie." That's my name. "Why do you call him Dickie?" the parents ask. "Because he's dickie colored," the little fool answers. They laugh. They laugh at how cute the little fool is.

But he's lying. He learned how to lie from my button eyes. He calls me "Dickie" because it's the baddest word he knows. And I'm the baddest wammerjammer monkey he will ever love.

He will rip me apart with his love. And he will grow big. He will be very big. And he will never forget me. And I'll love him forever like a bad monkey. Like a very bad monkey.

PENN JILLETTE

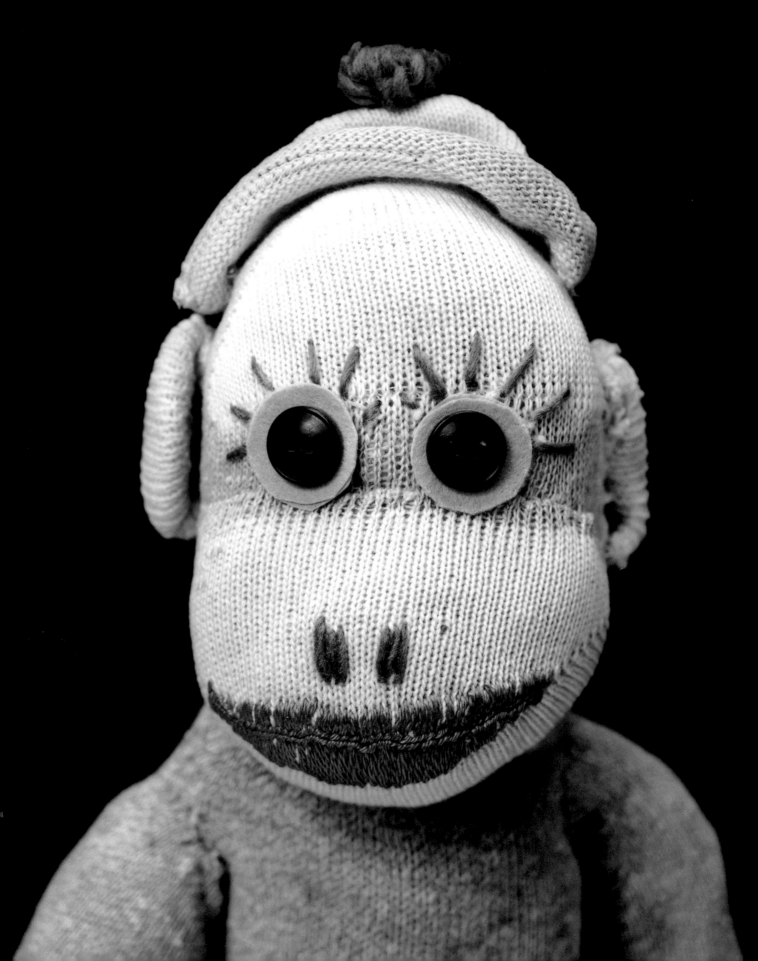

Sonya

She was born under a bad sign clutching a one-way ticket to trouble. Yes, Sonya was good-looking, so what! Good-looking broads were a dime a dozen in that one-horse border town where her mother ran the local house of pleasure. But Sonya had something more than those other girls—she had sizzle! By sixteen she was driving men wild; by seventeen she was driving her beaten-up Volvo to the big city, intent on stardom, or oblivion. She wasn't sure, and she didn't care.

She got herself an "agent," a bum called Lou with a gorilla-sized ego and a peanut addiction to match. Lou got Sonya some "classy" work, playing the burlesque houses down by the docks. She started to get quite a reputation: "Have you seen the new chick down at the Knitted Garter? She's a real looker, eyes dark as buttons!" "Sure! Name's Sonya. She's the hottie with the big, beautiful, tightly stuffed jowl and the mozzarella on her head. Everyone knows Sonya!" "Careful, she's dangerous."

Dangerous, schmangerous! Sonya did not care what people said. Let them talk! Sonya was living for kicks.

Soon she became top banana at the "Simian Sequin": she made money and she started spending it. Her favorite store was Yves Sock Laurent: that's where she found that gorgeous polka dot detachable collar with the velvet bow and the ricrac trim. "What a ricrac!" said Lou the first time she wore it. She rarely took it off.

Lou was devoted to Sonya, or at least to her money. Maybe that's why he took it all with him when he split. Sonya was devastated and hit the bottle hard. The night Lou left her she showed up late for work and fought with her pianist, Thelonious Monkey. The next day she was late again, and she got the boot. She was washed up with no way to pay the rent. Her life, and parts of her body, had unraveled. Sonya was on the skids.

These were dark years for Sonya. She even tried to end it all by throwing herself in the canal, but she floated. Fie on the synthetic batting!

One day a well-groomed lady stepped out of a limo and onto Sonya, who now lived in the gutter. Sonya knit her brow in consternation and squawked at the lady, who put on a large pair of red plastic bifocals and peered down. "You must be Sonya!" she said as she gathered the pitiful creature up in her caring arms.

Then, surprise, surprise, she took Sonya to a TV studio. What was happening? Was she being kidnapped? Why was this lady washing her in Woolite? Sonya looked at the TV monitor in the makeup room while an excitable fellow was rouging her copious lips, and she saw the vaguely familiar name Sally Jes . . .

Twenty minutes later Sonya and her parents were catching up on each others' lives over a tearful (virgin) banana daiquiri with three straws. Daddy had, he explained, left her and mummy to make his fortune when Sonya was just a little bit of stuffing. Once he made good, he tried to find his daughter and wife again, but they had moved with no forwarding address.

Sonya felt happy for the first time in her life: she realized that all she ever wanted was to be part of a tightly knit family, and now her dream had come true. Every stitch of it.

SIMON DOONAN

Earl

Sock monkeys are, without doubt, a very hardworking and patriotic segment of our society. But as with many of the world's displaced cultures, alcohol and dissolute living have taken a disproportionate toll on them, and, since they tend naturally toward joviality and mischief, it is not always easy to tell which ones are simply having fun, and which ones might become a danger to themselves and others. An experienced observer, however, can usually see the warning signs, and so can you, if you know what to look for.

The sock monkey depicted here—let us call him "Earl"—has abandoned all pretense of sobriety, making our study that much simpler.

Earl's eyes, if you look at them, are visibly glazed and unfocused, but more revealingly, notice how close to one another they are—the more sock monkeys drink, the closer together their eyes get. Not many people are aware of this; look for it next time you run into one. You may be surprised.

The drunken lassitude that Earl's posture communicates is not, you will further observe, restricted to his shoulders or arms, or even to the pronounced list of his party hat. Earl's very *ears* have lost their upright bearing and sag outward like thumbs.

Notice also what appears to be a small dropped stitch in Earl's mouth—so tiny and innocent at a glance, so easily overlooked—but this is all a sock monkey needs if it wishes to indulge its voracious appetite for whiskey and cigars. They are more easily opened than closed.

Once you know the telltale signs to watch for, you should have no problem spotting an intoxicated sock monkey. As a further precaution, however, you are reminded never to let a sock monkey operate a motorized vehicle in which you are a passenger or allow one to represent you in a court of law.

PETER GETTY

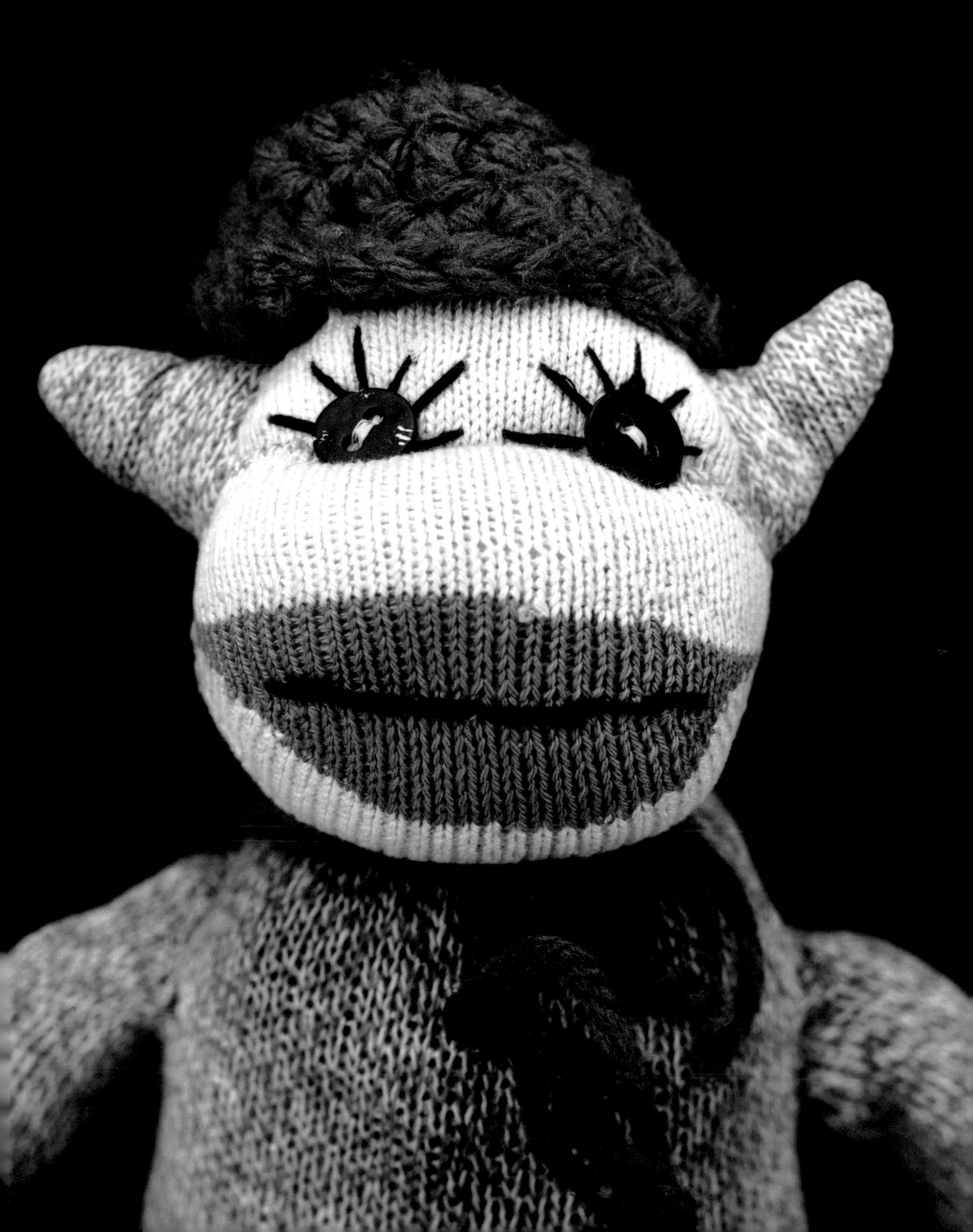

Meet MEEP Midge

I am a monkey. MEEP. Not a manatee. Not a mastodon. Not a mallard. Not a malodorous mink. Not a mamba, a marabou, a mantis, a mongoose, a mountain goat, nor mud puppy am I. MEEP. A monkey. I may mutter a mile-a-minute. Or MEEP mope in a mango tree. It all depends on my MEEPMEEPMEEEEEPMEEPMEEPMEEP mood. Which is never not improved by a MEEP mug of malted milk, some maple, and a mint. I am also partial to minestrone with matzo. Bananas? Only in moderation. I am one of many mammals in the order of Primates. MEEP meaning that, Missing Link and Man Ape-wise, we might be cousins, you and me. MEEP. My side of the family extends from slower-than-molasses lemurs down Madagascar way, to Great-aunt Macaque (that's "mekack"), who is a big muckety-muck in the Minneapolis Zoo. What a menagerie. I like a mishmash of music: medieval madrigals, Mozart, Thelonious Monk, Joni Mitchell, The Monkees, Madonna, Moby, the whole mélange played MEEP all at once, or in medley, by a maestro of the mandolin. It must be MEEEEEEEP mega-loud to be heard over my moped, when I take my baby sister Mathilda out for a spin. She's my minikin, my moppet. MEEP. She had the measles last May—the medicos cured her with meatballs—and she's been a maniac for MEEP macramé ever since. We like to dance the monkey minuet under the moon. No, I'm MEEP never mingy with the moola, especially when it comes to my feet: mukluks, moccasins, mules . . . I've got millions. Right now, I'm in mufti—which means I'm in my everyday clothes and not wearing any shoes at all. My favorite color is mauve. MEEP. No maize. MEEP. No magenta. MEEP. My mother was a matador, but since her maternity leave—and Mathilda—she MEEP manages a mackinaw manufactory. My father is the mind behind the macadamia nut macaroon. MEEP. My moniker? You can call me Midge, that's Monkey for "Migde." Will I ever stop saying meep? MEEP. Maybe.

INGRID SCHAFFNER

My Life

"My life? Hell, you don't want to hear about my life. Jesus, my throat is dry... A drink? Well, since you're buying and it's a hot day, sure. Why not. Just a little one. Maybe a beer. And a whiskey chaser. It's good to drink, on a hot day. Only problem with drinking is it makes me remember. And sometimes I don't want to remember. I mean, my mom: there was a woman. I never knew her as a woman but I seen photographs of her, before the operation. She said I needed a father, and seeing my own father had dumped her after he regained his eyesight (following a blow on the head from a Burmese cat that jumped from a penthouse apartment window and fell thirty stories, miraculously striking my father in exactly the right place to restore his sight, and then landing uninjured on the sidewalk, proving it's true what they say about cats always landing on their feet), claiming he had thought he was marrying her twin sister who looked completely different, but had, through a miracle of biology, exactly the same voice, which was why the judge granted the divorce—closed his eyes and even he couldn't tell them apart. So my father walked out a free man, and on the way from the court he was struck on the head by detritus falling from the sky; there was folks said it was lavatorial waste from a plane, although chemical examination revealed traces of elements unknown to science, and it said in the papers that the fecal matter contained alien proteins, but then it was hushed up. They took my father's body away for safekeeping. The government gave us a receipt though in a week it faded; I guess it was something in the ink, but that's another story. So then my mom announced I needed a man around the house and it was going to be her, and she worked a deal with that doctor so when the two of them won the Underwater Tango Contest he agreed to change her sex for nothing. Growing up I called her Dad and knew none of this. Nothing else interesting has ever happened to me. Another drink? Well, just to keep you company maybe, another beer, and don't forget the whiskey. Hey, make it a double. It isn't that I drink, but it's a hot day, and even when you're not a drinking man... You know, it was just such a day as this my wife dissolved. I'd read about the people who blew up, spontaneous combustion, that's the words. But Mary-Lou—that was my wife's name—we met the day she came out of her coma, seventy years asleep and hadn't aged a day; it's scary what ball lightning can do. And all the people on that submarine, like Mary-Lou, they all were froze in time, and after we were wed she'd visit them, sit by their bedsides, watch them while they slept. I drove a truck back then, and life was good. She coped well with the missing seven decades, and me, I like to think that if the dishwasher had not been haunted—well, possessed, I guess, would be more accurate—she'd still be here today. It preyed upon her mind, and the only exorcist that we could get turned out to be a midget from Utrecht and actually not a priest at all, for all he had was a candle, bell, and book. And by coincidence, the very day my wife, all haunted by the washer, deliquesced—went liquid in our bed—my truck was stole. That was when I left the States to travel 'round the world. And life's been dull as ditch water since then. Except... but no, my mind is going blank. My memory's been swallowed by the heat. Another drink? Well, sure..."

NEIL GAIMAN

The Veteran

I owe it to you little folks out there
to look my best. You pay good dough to see me.
I wear a rug in lieu of long-lost hair,
I rouge my lips and trim my nosehairs square.
When I am beautiful, you want to be me.

You know me from my one-hit wonder years,
when I was just a fuzzless juvenile,
aloft, spotlit, walking on screams and cheers
showered with pink and lacy souvenirs
from bobbysocks to nylons to argyle.

Those days my nights were lush with shocks and kicks.
And if I could, I would turn back the clock
to waste my life with lusty lunatics
and dance forever in a Motel Six
with a fishnet stocking and a white tube sock.

And yet, I'm glad to be here on the bench
of this fat old piano out of tune—
a whiskey-sotted cigarette-burned wench.
For out of her decrepit bones I'll wrench
the resurrection of this dead saloon.

White collar stiffs, you may think me bizarre.
But, pray, do not dismiss me with a smirk.
For when I play piano in this bar
I am these patrons' savior and their star—
while you get up at dawn and go to work.

It's not a real tie, true. It's on a clip.
Now sing along, and don't forget to tip.

                                    TELLER

Interview with the Chimp, Anne Z.

No. No I will not go to the party. I will stay in all night and I will not go to the party. I put these earrings on to wear to the party but I will not go to the party. They are new earrings—I bought them to wear to the party—but I will not go to the party. I am definitely not going to the party. Earrings or no earrings, blouse or no blouse, I will not go to the party. Yes, this blouse is new too. I thought it would be perfect for the party, but now it will never see the party because I am not going to the party. Wild horses couldn't drag me to the party. Earrings or no earrings, blouse or no blouse—do you like my blouse? Yes, I like it too. The shopgirl said the buttons brought out my eyes, the shopgirl said it would be *perfect* for the party, but blouse or no blouse, buttons or no buttons, eyes or no eyes, I will not go to the party. I will take off my blouse and take out my earrings and scrub the lipstick from my face because I am not going to the party. The lipstick is old. It is as old as my refusal to go to the party. You could almost say it's why I am not going to the party. I am not going to the party because my lipstick is not right for the party. And even if I succeed in scrubbing the lipstick from my face I still will not go to the party because my lipstick is not right for the party. It was for the very sake of the party that I first put on the lipstick. I put on the lipstick before I even knew of the party because even before I knew of the party I knew that one day there would be a party and that my lipstick would be perfect for it, but as it turns out my lipstick is not perfect for the party and so I will not go to the party. I will go to bed instead. I will go to bed but perhaps I will leave the lipstick on after all. I will go to bed with my lipstick on, and my blouse on too—my blouse that the shopgirl said would be perfect for the party—and I will dream about the party, and in my dream of the party a dashing gentle-simian will tell how the buttons of my blouse bring out my eyes and how my earrings perfectly accentuate my lipstick and how glad he is that I came to the party. But, I will tell him, I did not go to the party. I am not at the party. Or, rather, I am not at *the* party. I am at my party, and I am at it alone, and in the morning when they come to wake me up and tell me about the party I will say, Heavens! Was the party last night? And I did not go to it after all. Imagine that! I did not go to the party!

DALE PECK

O.r.i.o.n.

You were born cesarean section, too big for her slim body and, besides, a breech, meaning upside down and backwards. When they cut you out I was leaning over the anesthesiologist's shoulder to hold your mother's hands in mine.

Then the doctor told me that I had a son and I peeked inside the little plastic time capsule. Your long black hair was up and spiky, little eyes clenched shut like buttons and lips that were perfect porcelain duplicates of your mother's. I wanted to lift you and cradle you. I wanted to tell you something then but had no time to formulate the words.

"Your name, little monkey, is Bartholomew J. Zoiks. You will grow to be six feet four inches tall. You will live in Baltimore and Mississippi and you will favor gin martinis when you are old enough to order them. You were born in a cavern on the Island of Bermuda and your mother was a shipwrecked opera singer. Your father was a were-shark, a Prince from the Great Reef Kingdom of the Tiger Fins. Your grandparents on your mother's side were lost on an expedition to map the moon and your grandparents on your father's side live in the wilds of Tanzania where they search night and day for the lost Mangrove Apes who, legend has it, have two sets of opposable thumbs.

"You will have the delicate hands of a concert pianist and when you cross them above your head on your eighth birthday you will hear AM radio waves. You will study philosophy in school and realize (as we all have) that Marx stole from Hegel and Hegel from Marx. You will travel, trekking the Himalayas and sharpshooting flying fish over the Red Sea with a BB gun. There are many languages that you will hear but you will never learn to speak them and when you fall in love it will be with a quantum mathematician. You will live together in a garret apartment on the Ile Saint-Louis and there invent a new flavor of ice cream. Before you are a father yourself you will become many things—a mercenary, a superhero, a pirate, a race car driver, a dilettante, a raconteur extraordinaire."

And when you are old and I am young and we sit side by side on wooden deck chairs in the sea wind I will finally be able to explain to you the concept of infinity. How I am a minion and you are a minion and minions swim upstream together. You will tell me of your exploits. How you changed your name to Orion, the hunter's constellation, and where else I was wrong and where else I was right and all the many runes, maps, and secret signs you have learned. And you will tell me what I looked like to you then, that long slow moment when you became real not just because I wished you real, but because you wished for me.

M. RAVEN METZNER

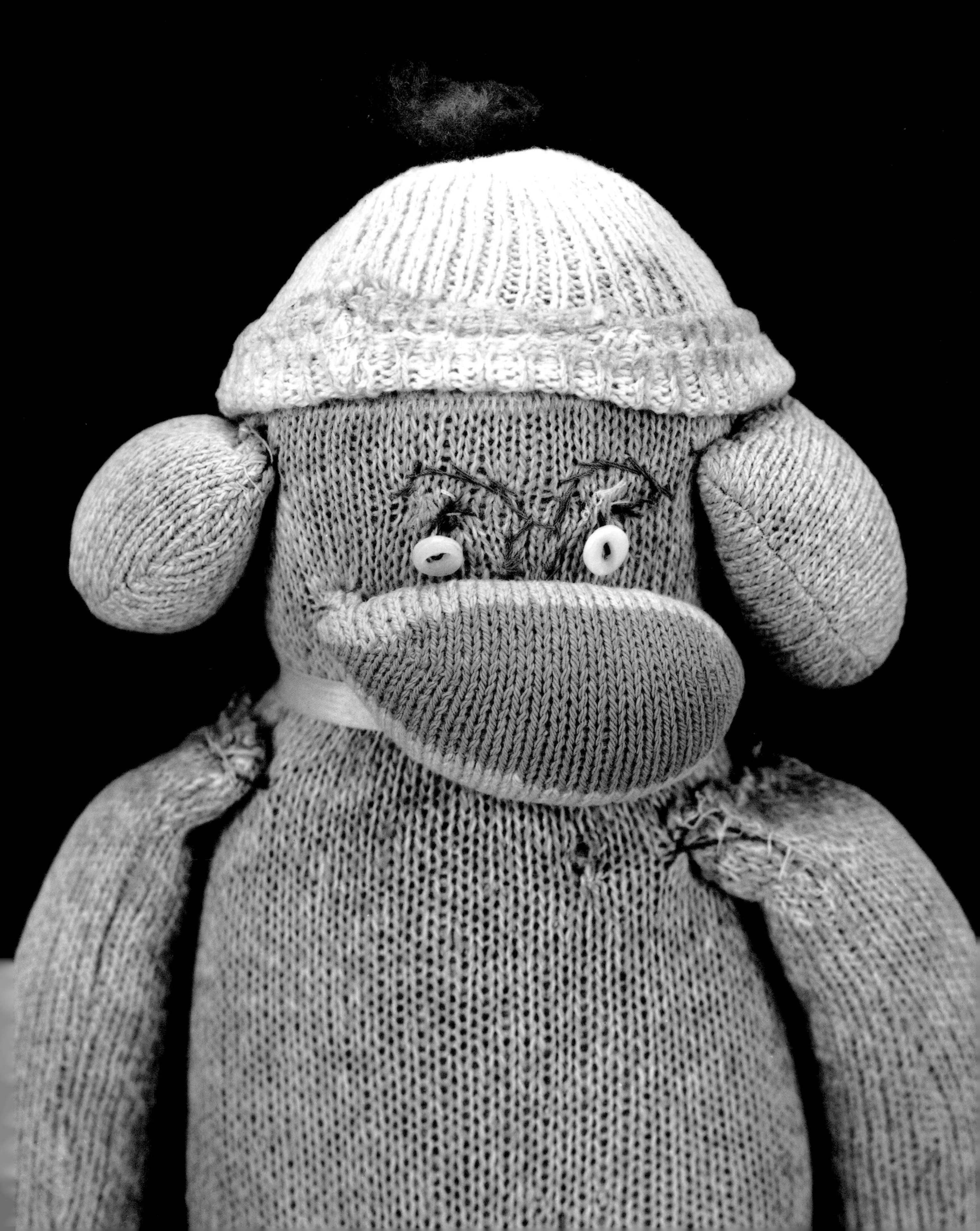

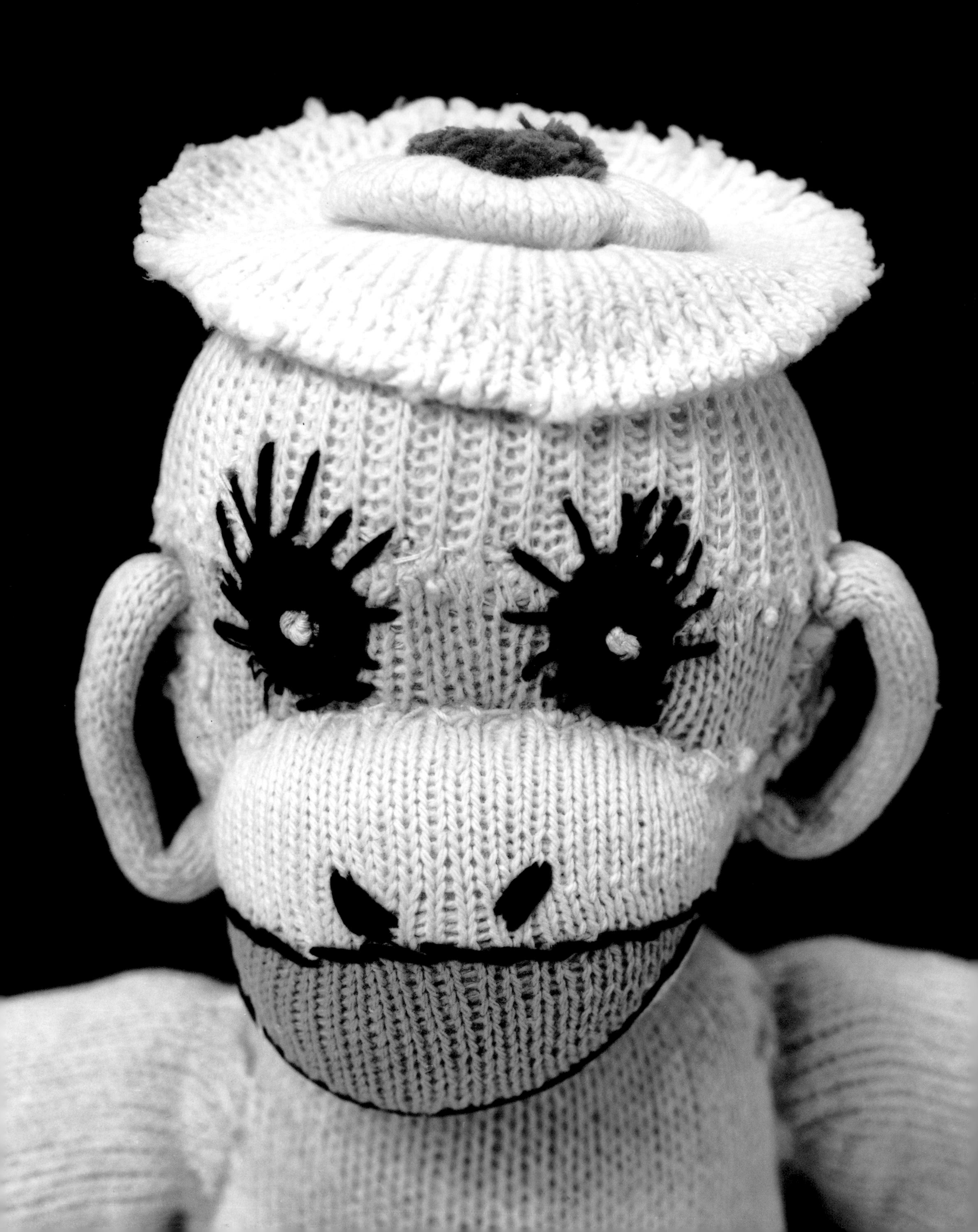

Bobo

I just got a call from someone named Deano. Deano, Deano. I saw him once at a parade without his shirt on—a furry, lumpy sock monkey. Deano called to tell me that he and my mate Coco are in love. I asked, "For how long?"

"Oh, six or seven months." Deano chattered on, where they met, what they do...

Now I feel so intensely sad, the feeling is almost wonder. My eyes widen because there's more and more to see. I must be the most lied-to sock monkey in San Francisco! I stay sitting where I am because it no longer matters where I am—this must be shock. Coco has turned my sweet little life into a big stupid melodrama in which I'm forced to play the part of the betrayed lover. The cliché becomes real: *"How could you treat me this way?"*

Now I'm starting to sizzle! I may be a monkey but I'm also a writer. I want to get back at my cheating mate for hurting me. How do you think I should do it?

ROBERT GLÜCK

Il fait plus froid ailleurs

I am not rich. I am not famous. I am not a genius, or even brilliant. Or stupid. I am not handsome. (But I am not ugly, either.) I am not without regrets or bad habits. I am not the kind of person to look at a painting and think: *It could not possibly be better.* I am not particularly tall or short or fat or skinny or shy or outgoing. I am not conspicuously uncoordinated. I am not, at the present moment, having a nervous breakdown. (But I am not untouched by anxiety, either.) I am not afraid of the dark, but given the choice, I prefer to fall asleep with the TV on. I am not Parisian. I am not someone who has been to Paris. I am not a great speaker of French, although there is a French phrase I sometimes say to myself when I'm walking in the cold without enough clothing on. I am not good at poker, and I am not thick-skinned. I am not conceited. I am not all that interested in architecture, or, for that matter, classical music. I am not outrageous. I am not afraid of needles. I am not a chocoholic. I am not the first to get to the party and I am not the last to leave. (And I am not the life of the party while I'm there.) I am not diligent about letter writing. I am not above the law. I am not badly missed. I am not a snorer and I am not from a prominent family. I am not as young as I used to be, which was not as young as I once upon a time was. I am not a smoker, but I smoke occasionally. I am not going to climb any tall mountains anytime soon. I am not tongue-tied or religious, paranoid, green-thumbed or asthmatic. I am not in love, or if I am in love, then love is not what I thought it would be. I am not a chimney sweep. I am not yesterday's news. Or today's. (And I am not going to be tomorrow's.) I am not dead, but I am not getting any younger, either. I am not bland. I am not made of money. I am not as regular a flosser as I would like to be. I am not kitschy, and I am not going to cry over spilt milk. I am not too proud to admit that life has dealt me many blows, that my life, thus far, has been a series of difficult obstacles. I am not afraid of flying. I am not a lemon-yellow blouse or uncooperative. I am not a good dancer, but I am not a bad one, either. I am not going to tell you that you are the most beautiful person in the world. Who is?

JONATHAN SAFRAN FOER

Madam Yakushova

Every day in class girls say to me, "Madam Yakushova, Madam Yakushova, show how to hold fan in Sleeping Beauty? Show us what is beautiful arabesque in Balanchine?" I say to girls, "Girls, I cannot show you how you be beautiful in ballet, whether Nijinska, or Tudor, or Balanchine. I can show how to be star. Your *job* to be beautiful, you must find art inside, what is beautiful inside and show to us."

When I was ballerina this we understood. No one had to tell us in Maryinsky School how to be beautiful. Ballet was not art in Soviet when I learn so many years ago. We had no choice. Must dance. Ballet was religion. Was higher than art. And lower. We were art and sexy at same time. No difference. Today there is difference between sexy dancing and art dancing. Too bad. This is why when first I defected to Europe through Ballet Russes, was no problem for people making dances. They were to show, not to bore, not to prove, it was delight. More like sport than art. And later when I moved to New York with Mr. B., had no problem making living. If no work that season came, dance job comes in revue in Greenwich Village. No difference between. There is music. There is someone telling, "Ludmilla Yakushova, you are violin so you do like violin, you do *tombé pas de bourrée, glissade, grand jeté, piqué arabesque,* dat dat dat, hold for applause." And so I do. In tutu or in cheesecake, don't matter.

Not important what happens before class. Life start in class. After when I finish class, performance begins. Woman begins. I start to buy pretty dresses. I start doing hair and chic makeups. I meet Andre in London and get marry. We have baby. I have to tell Georgie cannot do starring role in new Stravinsky ballet because of baby. I knew when I looked on her feet in delivery room she would not dance. I love her anyway. I love daughter more that she does not dance. She go to American college and become lawyer and not have to worry every day, "Oh I get fat, oh ugly costume, oh too mean choreographer."

Now I live in New York near to Lincoln Center. I give class every day. I see new girls dancing in new ways and I see choreographers thinking, thinking, thinking. Same as we. You never stop dancing till you do, then you STOP! Very sad to stop, very sad. But still I go to class in school. I wear makeup, I wear pretty rehearsal clothes, I wear bow at neck, bow in hair, pearls or earrings, or turban, something to show new girls to think about selves. Think on how they can be beautiful as me.

ISAAC MIZRAHI

WANTED

Wayne Lee Mandrill

Aliases: Bubba, Froggy the Gremlin, Ban Lon, Beano

Born in Sierra Leone, 1991. Escaped from Pfizer Laboratories, April, 1994. Caught working with illegal immigrant organ grinder, Venice, California, June, 1995. Sent to PrimaGen Laboratories, escaped from Liver Transplant Unit, September, 1996. Caught as stowaway on Dole refrigerator ship, October, 1997. Remanded to Eli Lilly Detention Facility where he developed a fentanyl habit during a self-injection experiment. Escaped in November, 1998. Last seen traveling with a Gypsy circus in Encino, California. Suspect may be found lurking in the vicinity of pharmacies or produce stands. May be wearing a hat and/or yellow beard.

He is to be considered long-armed and extremely gregarious.

GLENN O'BRIEN

CONTRIBUTORS

SIMON DOONAN is best known for his work as Creative Director of Barneys New York and for his weekly "Simon Says" column in *The New York Observer.* His autobiography, *Confessions of a Window Dresser,* was published in 1998. Doonan's next book, *Wacky Chicks; Women Without Borders,* will be published in spring 2003.

JONATHAN SAFRAN FOER was born in Washington, D.C., and now lives in Jackson Heights, Queens. He is the author of the novel *Everything Is Illuminated.*

NEIL GAIMAN is the author of the novel *American Gods* and the comic book *Sandman,* among others. He has won many awards and lives in the middle of America in a big, scary house. He usually needs a haircut.

PETER GETTY is a writer, businessman, and amateur sociologist who lives in San Francisco and Los Angeles.

ROBERT GLÜCK is a poet, critic, and fiction writer. His most recent novel was *Margery Kempe;* his next book, *Denny Smith,* is a collection of stories. He is an associate professor at San Francisco State University.

PENN JILLETTE is the bigger, louder half of Penn & Teller.

M. RAVEN METZNER is a feature screenwriter who was born, and still lives, in New York City. When he was a child, Raven's mother made him an adorable sock monkey with soulful button eyes and an infectious grin. He still has it.

ISAAC MIZRAHI is a three-time CFDA Award–winning fashion designer and a Drama Desk Award–winning costume designer. In addition to writing for various magazines, he hosts a TV talk/documentary show for the Oxygen Network.

GLENN O'BRIEN is a poet and essayist. His most recently published book is *Human Nature (dub version),* and the film *Downtown 81,* which he wrote and produced, was recently released on tape and DVD. He has a large collection of socks, but no monkeys.

DALE PECK is a novelist who lives in New York City. His works include *Martin and John; The Law of Enclosures;* and *Now It's Time to Say Goodbye.*

INGRID SCHAFFNER is a curator and writer about art. Some of the sock monkeys pictured in this book have been caught moonlighting in her traveling exhibition *Pictures, Patents, Monkeys, and More . . . On Collecting.*

TELLER is the smaller, quieter half of Penn & Teller.

ACKNOWLEDGMENTS

Special thanks to Deborah Aaronson, Doug Allen, Román Alonso, Abraham Axler, Nancy Benson, Max Blagg, Peter Bowen, AA Bronson, Sam Brown, Charles Burkhalter, Clifford Chase, Tory Dent, Paul Di Filippo, Lisa Eisner, Lila Selene Glantzman-Leib, Tracy Granger, Sean Harvey, Gene Hatcher, Elizabeth Hayt, Donald Kennison, Jim Knipfel, Mark Krayenhoff, Anna Louise Kuoni Oakes, Laura Lindgren, Marcia Lucas, Ethan Mack, Hannah Mack, Joshua Mack, Joan Murphy, Melissa Holbrook Pierson, Eliza Rockefeller, Tor Seidler, Grace Yu Ying Smith, Jorge Socarras, Evelyn Svenson, Ken Swezey, Rhys Tivey, Martha Warren, Ron & Carol Wright, and the anonymous creators of these sock monkeys.

sock monkeys (200 out of 1,863)
Photographs © 2002 by Arne Svenson. All rights reserved.

ISBN 0-9722111-2-8

Designed by Laura Lindgren

Ideal World Books
Available through D.A.P./Distributed Art Publishers
155 Sixth Avenue, 2nd Floor, New York, NY 10013
telephone (212) 627-1999 · fax (212) 627-9484
www.artbook.com

Printed in China
First Edition
10 9 8 7 6 5 4 3 2 1